people in the NEWS

Barack Obama

by Sherri and Mark Devaney

LUCENT BOOKS

An imprint of Thomson Gale, a part of The Thomson Corporation

THOMSON

GALE

Detroit • New York • San Francisco • New Haven, Conn. • Waterville, Maine • London

© 2007 Thomson Gale, a part of The Thomson Corporation.

Thomson and Star Logo are trademarks and Gale and Lucent Books are registered trademarks used herein under license.

For more information, contact
Lucent Books
27500 Drake Rd.
Farmington Hills, MI 48331-3535
Or you can visit our Internet site at http://www.gale.com

LIBRARY OF CONGRESS CATALOGING-IN-PUBLICATION DATA

Devaney, Sherri.
    Barack Obama / by Sherri and Mark Devaney.
        p. cm. — (People in the news)
    Includes bibliographical references and index.
    Audience: Grades 5-8.
    ISBN-13: 978-1-59018-937-5 (hardcover : alk. paper)
    ISBN-10: 1-59018-937-X (hardcover : alk. paper)
    1. Obama, Barack—Juvenile literature. 2. Legislators—United States—Biography—Juvenile literature. 3. African American legislators—Biography—Juvenile literature. 4. United States. Congress. Senate—Biography—Juvenile literature. 5. Racially mixed people—United States—Biography—Juvenile literature. I. Devaney, Mark. II. Title.
    E901.1.O23D488 2007
    973'.04960730092—dc22
    [B]
                                                                        2006021945

Printed in the United States of America

Contents

F ame and celebrity are alluring. People are drawn to those who walk in fame's spotlight, whether they are known for great accomplishments or for notorious deeds. The lives of the famous pique public interest and attract attention, perhaps because their experiences seem in some ways so different from, yet in other ways so similar to, our own.

Newspapers, magazines, and television regularly capitalize on this fascination with celebrity by running profiles of famous people. For example, television programs such as *Entertainment Tonight* devote all of their programming to stories about entertainment and entertainers. Magazines such as *People* fill their pages with stories of the private lives of famous people. Even newspapers, newsmagazines, and television news frequently delve into the lives of well-known personalities. Despite the number of articles and programs, few provide more than a superficial glimpse at their subjects.

Lucent's People in the News series offers young readers a deeper look into the lives of today's newsmakers, the influences that have shaped them, and the impact they have had in their fields of endeavor and on other people's lives. The subjects of the series hail from many disciplines and walks of life. They include authors, musicians, athletes, political leaders, entertainers, entrepreneurs, and others who have made a mark on modern life and who, in many cases, will continue to do so for years to come.

These biographies are more than factual chronicles. Each book emphasizes the contributions, accomplishments, or deeds that have brought fame or notoriety to the individual and shows how that person has influenced modern life. Authors portray their subjects in a realistic, unsentimental light. For example, Bill Gates— the cofounder and chief executive officer of the software giant Microsoft—has been instrumental in making personal computers the most vital tool of the modern age. Few dispute his business savvy, his perseverance, or his technical expertise, yet critics say he is ruthless in his dealings with competitors and driven more by his desire to maintain Microsoft's dominance in the computer industry than by an interest in furthering technology.

In these books, young readers will encounter inspiring stories about real people who achieved success despite enormous obstacles. Oprah Winfrey—the most powerful, most watched, and wealthiest woman on television today—spent the first six years of her life in the care of her grandparents while her unwed mother sought work and a better life elsewhere. Her adolescence was colored by promiscuity, pregnancy at age fourteen, rape, and sexual abuse.

Each author documents and supports his or her work with an array of primary and secondary source quotations taken from diaries, letters, speeches, and interviews. All quotes are footnoted to show readers exactly how and where biographers derive their information and provide guidance for further research. The quotations enliven the text by giving readers eyewitness views of the life and accomplishments of each person covered in the People in the News series.

In addition, each book in the series includes photographs, annotated bibliographies, timelines, and comprehensive indexes. For both the casual reader and the student researcher, the People in the News series offers insight into the lives of today's newsmakers—people who shape the way we live, work, and play in the modern age.

Barack Obama: Taking the Stage

On the evening of July 27, 2004, at the Democratic National Convention in Boston, a man named Barack Obama Jr. delivered the keynote address and ascended into the American spotlight. While many people familiar with politics already knew of Obama, most people outside Washington, D.C., and Illinois—Obama's own state—were unaware of the youthful politician with the unusual name.

The speech, which Obama wrote himself, riveted the nation, and he has since become one of the rising stars of the Democratic Party. Republicans realized immediately that they would have to contend with Obama's sudden popularity, undeniable charisma, and impressive intellect. Clearly, he was a new breed of Democrat who held untold promise as a leader.

In some ways his selection as a keynote speaker at the convention signified that the nation itself had changed. Obama's odd name, mixed race, and lack of political experience—things that may have kept him from reaching such a lofty stage in past decades—no longer mattered. In fact, his presence at the convention had less to do with the past and everything to do with the future. At the time, Obama was a candidate for senator of Illinois; he went on to easily win election, buoyed by the explosion of attention he received as a result of his now-famous speech. Almost overnight he became a sensation, and talk of his potential has continued ever since.

*Barack Obama gives the keynote address at the 2004
Democratic National Convention.*

Nowhere but America

Yet while there is conjecture about Obama as a possible presidential or vice-presidential candidate, he remains an enigma. Many people are curious about who he is and where he came from. Compared to that of many political candidates, whose every move from youth to adulthood has been carefully scripted and recorded, Obama's upbringing and path to prominence have been somewhat haphazard and even a bit mysterious.

The story of Obama's rise to prominence is uniquely American.

Still, in many ways, the fact that his father was an African from Kenya and his mother a middle-class white woman from Kansas explains in part why he has been able to appeal to widely diverse cultures. Indeed, because of his mixed heritage Obama has encountered both obstacles and opportunities that few American political candidates have ever faced. And despite his perceived weaknesses, Obama's stature has steadily grown in parallel with his experience as a new leader in the U.S. Senate. Throughout each period in his life—as a student, a community organizer, a lawyer, a state legislator, and a senator—Obama has been able to learn, grow, and succeed, winning supporters along the way.

When he addressed the nation and the world at the Democratic National Convention, he stated, "In no other country on earth is my story even possible."[1] He is right. His story could take place only in the United States, a country where diversity and opportunity are embraced and enabled by a democratic system that provides equality for all people, even those who do not seem to have a chance of success. Today, Obama stands as a sort of living symbol for what is best about the nation, namely that through hard work and scholarship anyone can achieve his or her dreams. On the other hand, even Obama would admit that he has been blessed with good fortune and it is entirely possible that his luck could run out, especially as his opponents in the Republican Party become more of a force to be reckoned with.

Only time will tell what Obama will do next, but in the meantime a review of the high and low points of his episodic life and career reveals his beliefs and actions, which have shaped his unique persona and inspiring worldview. A deeper exploration of the man explains his remarkable ability to overcome adversity. It becomes apparent how he has become synonymous with the subject he loves to talk about to audiences around the country—hope.

Chapter 1

A Fateful Beginning

Many political leaders are born into families that possess wealth, connections to powerful people, and a cultural background that reflects mainstream America. And then there is Barack Obama, who grew up humbly, without friends or family in high places, and, most notably, came from an improbable mix of cultures. Yet despite the fact that he does not fit the mold of a typical politician, Obama is considered by many to be one of the most interesting and dynamic figures to emerge on the American political scene in the last thirty years.

Obama's ancestry as well as his unique personal history explain why he has been able to appeal to a broad spectrum of the populace and gain a growing reputation as a man who can bring people together and perhaps change the United States as well as the world. Indeed, there are a lot of expectations for Obama. Few people dispute the fact that he has the talent, knowledge, and character to accomplish great things, and a look at his past shows that he has already endured circumstances that would have prevented many other people from achieving success.

Two Vastly Different Worlds

Barack Obama Jr. is the son of two people from vastly different parts of the world. His father, Barack Obama Sr., was from Kenya, born a member of the Luo tribe on the shores of Lake Victoria in a place called Alego. His mother, S. Ann Dunham, was born in Kansas.

A bright child, Barack Obama Sr. went from tending goats on his father's farm to earning a sponsorship to attend a university in the United States. In 1959, at the age of twenty-three, he became the University of Hawaii's first African student. It was there that he met eighteen-year-old Dunham, who was also a student at the university.

Dunham was a shy but smart only child. She was actually named Stanley Ann, after her father, Stanley Dunham, a man whose interests and energy led their small family to move around the country frequently as he sought better jobs and a better way of life. Born and raised in Kansas, Stanley Dunham (or "Gramps," as young Barack called him) was a soldier in World War II who never experienced combat. Ann was born at the army base where he was stationed. Upon his return to civilian life, he enrolled at the University of California at Berkeley under the GI bill, which provided tuition to military veterans. However, according to Barack in his memoir, *Dreams from My Father: A Story of Race and Inheritance*, "the classroom couldn't contain his ambitions."[2] So

Born into Kenya's Luo tribe (members are pictured here), Barack Obama Sr. would later attend the University of Hawaii as the school's first African student.

the family moved again, first back to Kansas, then through a series of small Texas towns, and eventually to Seattle, where they stayed long enough for Ann to finish high school.

During that time, Stanley Dunham worked as a furniture salesman. One day he learned from his manager that the furniture company was opening a new store in Honolulu. That bit of news led to a fateful decision to move in 1959, this time off the mainland of the United States to a so-called island paradise where, Dunham believed, an enterprising young man could make his mark. Barack describes his grandfather's character: "He would always be like that, my grandfather, always searching for that new start, always running away from the familiar. . . . His was an

Loving v. Virginia

Although civil rights were expanded in the United States during the 1960s, interracial marriage was by no means easily accepted. If Ann Dunham and Barack Obama Sr. had met on the mainland of the United States, they might not have married. In many states it was still illegal for whites and blacks to marry. And in the southern states at the time, it would have been likely that Barack's father could have been harmed, even hanged, by an angry mob that would have taken violent offense to a black man having a relationship with a white woman.

In fact, it was not until Barack was six years old that the U.S. Supreme Court declared Virginia's antimiscegenation statute, the Racial Integrity Act of 1924, unconstitutional in the case of *Loving v. Virginia*, which legally ended all race-based restrictions on marriage in the United States. At the time such laws were ruled unconstitutional, sixteen states still had laws prohibiting interethnic marriage. Despite the ruling, such laws existed unenforced in several states until November 2000, when Alabama became the last state to repeal its law.

Obama (pictured in 2004) is the product of a mixed-race marriage, a union strongly opposed by his paternal grandfather, Hussein.

American character, one typical of men of his generation, men who embraced the notion of freedom and individualism and the open road."[3]

Despite Stanley Dunham's ambitions, he never got rich. His wife, Madelyn, whose nickname was "Toot," also worked. She took a job in a bank and rose up in the ranks through dint of diligent professionalism. In fact, when Stanley experienced low points in business, Madelyn kept the family afloat financially.

Cultures Collide

Although the Dunhams never prospered, they were open-minded parents who provided Ann with a stable home. That tolerance was tested, however, when eighteen-year-old Ann informed them that she wanted to marry a twenty-three-year-old black man from another continent. Yet neither Stanley nor Madelyn could deny that Ann was truly in love, and Barack Obama Sr.'s intellect and charm quickly won them over.

Barack Obama Sr.'s father, Hussein, was less agreeable to the match. Shortly before the wedding, he wrote a letter to Stanley Dunham from Africa saying that he did not approve of the marriage. One reason for this, according to Barack's mother, was that Hussein did not want the Obama blood to be "sullied by a white woman."[4] Barack Obama Sr. wrote back to Hussein informing him that he was going forward with the wedding, and he married Ann in a small civil ceremony in 1960. Barack Hussein Obama Jr. was born shortly thereafter on August 4, 1961.

Barack Obama Sr. continued with his education, and upon graduation from the University of Hawaii with a degree in economics that he had earned in only three years, he received two scholarships for graduate school. One was from the New School in New York City and would have provided him with full tuition, along with room and board for Ann and the baby. The second scholarship, from Harvard, provided only full tuition for Obama Sr. According to Barack's mother, Ann, while deciding which offer to accept, Obama Sr. received harsh news from his father. Hussein was adamant in his rejection of Ann. He threatened to have his son's student visa revoked, which would have forced Obama Sr. to return to Africa before completing his graduate studies. The pressure from Hussein, coupled with his own overwhelming desire to attend a university as prestigious as Harvard, led Obama Sr. to choose the Ivy League school. He left for Massachusetts in 1963 to pursue his studies. Ann remained in Hawaii with their two-year-old son. The couple separated and eventually divorced.

Thus, early in his life, before he was even aware of it, Obama was different from other children in many ways. Half black, half white, and essentially fatherless, he already could not be neatly categorized into one demographic or class.

Lessons from Indonesia

Barack Obama Jr.'s life soon took another turn. About two years after the senior Obama left, Ann met Lolo Soetoro, a University of Hawaii student from Indonesia, a Southeast Asian country comprising several islands in the Indian and Pacific Oceans. After dating Soetoro for two years, Ann accepted his proposal of marriage. Soon after the couple married, Soetoro returned to his homeland, but unlike Barack Obama Sr., he took his new bride and her now six-year-old son with him. Barack, who was called "Barry" as a child, lived in Indonesia for four years. There, his mother gave birth to his half sister, Maya.

While living in Indonesia, Barack came to understand how the United States, unlike many other countries, offers numerous

Living in Indonesia in the 1960s, young Obama was moved by the plight of the country's poor, who had little chance of improving their lot.

opportunities as an economically free society. Even as a young child, he observed that people in Indonesia are born into families whose lot in life is dictated by their economic class, and it is extremely difficult to ascend into a higher economic class. In the United States, by contrast, all people have the freedoms of life, liberty, and the pursuit of happiness regardless of their race, gender, or class.

Barack was also exposed to abject poverty in Indonesia, where many families struggled daily to obtain enough food. People lived modestly in ramshackle homes where it was common to see chickens and livestock roaming in yards. Later in life, Obama drew parallels between what he witnessed in Indonesia and what he witnessed in American inner cities.

During his time in Indonesia, Barack also began to learn about his African American heritage. His mother regularly provided him

Obama attended prep school in Hawaii at the prestigious Punahou Academy.

with reading materials about the treatment of African Americans in the United States. She taught him about the nation's history of slavery and the more recent fight for civil rights. She made sure that her son knew of the great contributions made by black leaders in politics, history, culture, music, and sports. Barack describes her message in his memoir: "To be black was to be the beneficiary of a great inheritance, a special destiny, glorious burdens that only we were strong enough to bear."[5]

But the pride his mother passed on to young Barack was tempered by his growing awareness of issues surrounding race. Most disturbing was the self-hatred among some African Americans due to their skin color. Barack came upon the subject while reading a *Life* magazine story about a black man who had tried to peel off his skin to look white. It had never occurred to Barack that people would feel so ashamed of their skin color that they would take such drastic and dangerous steps to undo nature, but the article changed his understanding of race. He explains in his memoir, "I began to notice . . . that there was nobody like me in the Sears, Roebuck Christmas catalog that Toot and Gramps sent us, and that Santa was a white man. . . . I still trusted my mother's love—but I now faced the prospect that her account of the world, and my father's place in it, was somehow incomplete."[6]

Punahou Academy

After four years of living in Indonesia, Barack was sent back to Hawaii to live with his grandparents and enter the fifth grade at Punahou Academy, an elite Hawaiian prep school. His grandparents were only too happy to accommodate him. They were proud that their grandchild was a student at such a well-respected educational institution.

Having been away from the United States for so long, Barack felt out of place at Punahou. The majority of other students had attended school together since kindergarten. Most of them came from well-to-do families and had better quality and more stylish clothes than Barack. He was one of only two black children in his class, and other students mocked his foreign name. Instead of feeling proud of his Kenyan heritage, Barack often felt conflicted, even embarrassed by his differences from the other children.

As Barack sought to fit in among his classmates, he received some startling news. Barack Obama Sr. had been in a serious car accident in Kenya, and he was coming for a month-long visit to recuperate after a lengthy stay in the hospital.

Tense Visit

The young Barack was nervous about meeting his father. His mother and grandparents had told him that his father was a brilliant diplomat doing important work to help his country, but young Barack still felt he knew little about him and struggled with his absence. Sometimes he felt proud that his father was a leader in Kenya trying to improve life for his countrymen. But at other times, Barack could not understand why his father was not with him.

The visit was awkward and confusing. Young Barack was impressed with his father, but the man was a stranger to him. The boy knew that his father was intelligent and worldly, but he was also strict, criticizing his son for watching too much television and for not studying more. Education had been the key to Barack Obama Sr.'s escaping an impoverished life. Young Barack was not as desperate to learn as his father had been, and this led to tension during their brief encounter.

The elder Barack's visit created tension for his son in another way as well. Young Barack had grown up different, a black child being raised by white grandparents in a state populated by Hawaiians. He feared that being exposed as the son of an African who spoke with a strange accent would only emphasize the contrast between himself and other children in Hawaii.

One event in particular characterized the conflicted emotions that Barack had for his father. When Barack's teacher learned that Barack's father was in Hawaii, she invited him to speak to her class. Barack dreaded the day because he expected his classmates to tease him afterward. His fear turned to pride, however, as the man from Africa held the students transfixed. Barack describes what happened:

Triumphs and Tragedy

When Barack Obama Sr. returned to Africa, he married a white woman whose father worked in the Kenyan embassy. For some time he did well working for an American oil company. Kenya gained its independence from England in 1963, and Obama Sr. was connected with all the top government people, which led him to take a high-ranking job with the Ministry of Tourism.

Obama Sr. was still with the Ministry of Tourism in 1966, when a division grew between two Kenyan tribes: the Kikuyu, led by President Jomo Kenyatta, and the Luo, Obama Sr.'s tribe. The Luo tribe complained that Kikuyu tribe members were getting the best jobs in the country, and Obama Sr. protested publicly about the issue. His outspokenness caused him to be banished from the government. His passport was revoked, so he could not leave Kenya to find other opportunities abroad. During this time, his wife left him. He began to drink and fell into near poverty for many years.

Eventually the political situation in Kenya changed, and Obama Sr. was able to return to government work in the Ministry of Finance. Tragically, just as his life was beginning to improve, he was killed suddenly in a car accident in 1982, when Obama Jr. was twenty-one.

He spoke of the wild animals that still roamed the plains, the tribes that still required a young boy to kill a lion to prove his manhood. . . . He told us of Kenya's struggle to be free, how the British had wanted to stay and unjustly rule the people, just as they had in America; how they had been enslaved only because of the color of their skin, just as they had in America; but that Kenyans . . . longed to be free and develop themselves through hard work and sacrifice.[7]

Barack's father stayed for only one month. Soon after he returned to Africa, Barack's mother, now separated from Lolo, came back to Hawaii to pursue a master's degree in anthropology. Barack lived in an apartment a block from the Punahou Academy with his mother and his sister, Maya, for the next three years.

Teenage Struggles with Identity

When his mother made plans to return to Indonesia once again—this time to complete her fieldwork for her graduate degree—Barack elected to stay at Punahou and to once again live with his grandparents. During these years Barack's internal conflicts about his identity grew. His mixed heritage created conflict when he befriended blacks who voiced their resentment of whites. He was privy to such comments because those who made them did not know that his mother was white. In an interview with talk-show host Oprah Winfrey, Obama describes his inner turmoil:

Obama described his ambivalence about his mixed-race background during an interview with talk show host Oprah Winfrey (pictured).

There was a level of . . . a divided identity. One that was inside the home and one was to the outside world. . . . And I think it was reconciling those two things, the understanding that I can be African American and proud of that heritage and proud of that culture and part of that community and yet not be limited by it. And that . . . that's not exclusive of my love for my mother or my love for my grandparents, that I can be part of the same thing.[18]

Barack's personal conflicts along with typical teen rebelliousness led him to wayward behavior. He drank, smoked marijuana, and even used cocaine. Although he never became addicted to hard drugs, he did develop a cigarette smoking habit that would plague him for years.

Barack also sought refuge on the basketball court. He made the team at Punahou his last two years of high school and helped win a state title. He describes how he found acceptance and belonging, first playing pickup basketball in park playgrounds near his home and then as a member of his high school basketball team. He recalls, "I was living out a caricature of black male adolescence, itself a caricature of swaggering American manhood. . . . At least on the basketball court I could find a community of sorts, with an inner life all its own. It was there that I would make my closest white friends, on turf where blackness couldn't be a disadvantage."[9] As Barack spent more time on social activities than academics, his grades suffered a bit, and so did his ambition. He drifted without clear direction as his high school years concluded.

Occidental College

Despite his lack of focus on his future, Obama wound up at Occidental College in Los Angeles in 1979. The criteria he used to pick the school could be construed as a whim. He chose Occidental because he had heard of the school from a girl vacationing in Hawaii from Brentwood, a Los Angeles suburb.

At Occidental, he once again grappled with issues of race. Unlike the black students from economically depressed cities,

Students sit on the library steps at Columbia University, where Obama became a student in 1981.

Obama could not easily identify with the plight of impoverished and disadvantaged blacks in the United States. In fact, he reflects in his memoir that he was more like "the black students who had grown up in the suburbs, kids whose parents had already paid the price of escape"[10] from inner cities. His multiracial makeup compounded his sense of estrangement from blacks, yet he was not comfortable downplaying or even disavowing his African American heritage as some multiracial students did.

In a state of limbo between black and white, Obama describes how his friends were the more politically active black students. The foreign students. The Chicanos. The Marxist professors and structural feminists and punk-rock performance poets. We smoked cigarettes and wore leather jackets. . . . When we ground out our cigarettes in the hallway carpet or set our stereos so loud that the walls began to shake, we were resisting bourgeois society's stifling constraints. We weren't indifferent or careless or insecure. We were alienated.[11]

Yet once again, Barack reached a crossroads. On one hand, he tried to assimilate what he presumed to be black thinking—rebel against white authority, even if it means doing poorly in college, because for blacks school does not matter. However, he also encountered blacks who appreciated the sacrifices that their families had made to send them to school, and they criticized him for not applying himself academically. Writer and reporter Noam Scheiber states, "Obama's eventual response to his multicultural background was neither to shun his black identity, nor to shore it up by segregating himself from whites. It was to be racially proud, while striving to succeed in mainstream (and predominantly white) institutions."[12]

Eventually, Obama came to the realization that he was not living up to his full potential. After two years at Occidental, he transferred to Columbia University in 1981. His childhood and adolescence over, Obama set out to find his calling in New York City.

Chapter 2

The Streets of Chicago

As a young adult Barack Obama made a series of career moves that were impressive yet unexpected. He arrived at Columbia University eager to live in what he called "a true city, with black neighborhoods in close proximity."[13] He got his wish because the school is located only a few blocks from Harlem, a section of New York City that is home to thousands of African Americans and is rife with all the societal ills common to urban areas: poverty, drugs, violence, and homelessness.

By the time Obama completed his degree in political science with a specialization in international relations in 1983, he had decided to become a community organizer. He wanted to bring people together on a local level to promote social progress and protest unfair treatment, which could include anything from poor educational facilities, inferior housing conditions, and pollution to lost jobs and low wages for working-class citizens. According to Obama, "Communities had never been a given in this country. . . . Communities had to be created, fought for, tended like gardens."[14]

Time for Change

Despite the fact that American citizens in inner cities had many problems, it was not so simple for Obama to find work as a community organizer. He submitted letters to many civil rights organizations and to black elected officials all over the country who had progressive agendas, yet no one replied.

To earn an income in the meantime, he took a research assistant job at a consulting house for a multinational corporation. He was eventually promoted to the position of financial writer. Obama

Obama was pleased with the proximity of Columbia University to Harlem, a largely black New York City neighborhood (pictured in 1986).

now had money, his own office, and his own secretary. He describes this time in his life in his memoir:

> Sometimes coming out of an interview with Japanese finan-
> ciers or German bond traders, I would catch my reflection
> in the elevator doors—see myself in a suit and tie, a brief-
> case in my hand—and for a split second I would imagine
> myself as a captain of industry, barking out orders, closing
> the deal, before I remembered who it was that I had told
> myself I wanted to be and felt pangs of guilt for my own lack
> of resolve.[15]

This guilt eventually resulted in Obama resigning his position and focusing again on finding work as a community organizer. Although he got a job organizing a conference on drugs, unemployment, and housing, this role was too removed from the streets. So he took another position, this time in Harlem, trying to convince the students at City College of the importance of recycling. Then he took another low-paying assignment passing out flyers for an assemblyman's race in Brooklyn. "In six months I was broke, unemployed, eating soup from a can,"[16] he recalls. But finally an opportunity came to him that literally redirected his life.

Finding a Focus in Chicago

Obama was recruited by a labor organizer affiliated with the Calumet Community Religious Conference (CCRC), an organization formed to address the impact of factory closings and layoffs then taking place in South Chicago. Once critical to the nation's economy, Chicago's manufacturing companies, like so many others around the nation, had relocated operations—mostly overseas to take advantage of cheaper labor—or had simply gone out of business. The CCRC sought to mobilize residents through a network of twenty-eight suburban and urban churches, known as the Developing Communities Project. The objective was to bring jobs and manufacturing back to Chicago, and Obama was hired at a small annual salary in 1985 to help unite people in this common cause.

Obama worked with the CCRC in Chicago (pictured) to confront the issues of factory closings and layoffs in the city.

Obama found that his job was not easy. For one, he discovered that it was difficult to convince local black religious leaders to agitate for more and better jobs for African Americans, mainly because the mayor of Chicago at the time was Harold Washington, the first African American ever elected to that position. Washington

When the CCRC tried to increase job opportunities for blacks in Chicago, black church leaders—worried about appearing disrespectful to Chicago's popular black mayor, Harold Washington (center)—did not want to help.

was a hero to Chicago's African Americans, and some of the church leaders did not want to be perceived as disrespectful to him.

Despite the reluctance of some of the church leaders to cooperate, Obama pressed on with a variety of issues that strayed somewhat from the mission of the DCP. For example, he held a meeting to address gang violence, but the organized event flopped. Hardly anyone showed up. Obama learned that gang violence was too big an issue to rally people around. While people certainly wanted something to be done to improve safety in their neighborhoods, they most wanted help finding jobs. Obama learned a valuable lesson: If he was going to succeed at community organizing, he had to focus on concrete matters such as jobs and decent housing for the working poor. Sometime thereafter he found a place to concentrate his efforts: Altgeld Gardens.

Altgeld Gardens and MET

Obama realized his first real success as a community organizer by helping to call the attention of the Mayor's Office of Employment and Training (MET) to Altgeld Gardens, a public housing project on the southern edge of the city of Chicago. Unlike high-rise projects common to most major cities, Altgeld was only two stories tall, and although the residents did not own their apartments, they took pride in their homes, despite the deplorable conditions in and around them. Obama describes Altgeld:

> The Altgeld Gardens Public Housing Project sat at Chicago's southernmost edge: two thousand apartments arranged in a series of two-story brick buildings with army-green doors and grimy mock shutters. . . . To the east . . . was the Lake Calumet landfill, the largest in the Midwest. And to the north, directly across the street, was the Metropolitan Sanitary District's sewage treatment plant. . . . The stench, the toxins, the empty uninhabited landscape. For close to a century, the few square miles surrounding Altgeld had taken in the offal of scores of factories, the price people had paid for their high-wage jobs. Now that the jobs were gone, and those people that could had already left, it seemed only natural to use the land as a dump. A dump—and a place to house poor blacks.[17]

Obama interviewed and befriended residents of Altgeld. He learned that employment was a key issue for them, and he set out to connect the group with MET, which referred unemployed people to training programs throughout the city. He discovered that MET did not have an office anywhere near Altgeld, so he wrote to the woman in charge of the agency. She agreed to meet with a group of Altgeld Gardens residents. Obama's demand was for a job intake and training center on the far south side of the city. He coached the residents on what to say at the meeting and made all the arrangements for it. More than one hundred people attended the event, and the director of MET could not deny that an office needed to be established in the community.

Asbestos at Altgeld

Emboldened by his triumph with MET, Obama's next challenge involved helping Altgeld residents persuade the city of Chicago to fix a problem with asbestos. Asbestos was once considered a useful product because it is fireproof. For decades asbestos was used to insulate pipes and walls in buildings and homes until it was discovered to cause cancer. A woman who lived in the Altgeld housing project showed Obama a small advertisement she had found seeking contractors to remove asbestos from an Altgeld management office site. The woman wondered if the apartments had asbestos as well.

Obama led a small contingent of residents to the building manager's office and was told that the apartments had been tested and that there was no asbestos in them. When pressed for evidence, the building manager could not deliver proof of this testing. In response, Obama and some Altgeld residents organized a bus trip to the Community Housing Authority's offices.

Obama notified the press to attend the meeting because he knew that the news media would be interested in a story about the possibility of a known cancer-causing material such as asbestos having a negative impact on the health of city residents. He was also confident that Community Housing Authority executives would not want to be portrayed publicly as negligent. Sure enough, with cameras rolling, they admitted that asbestos was present in the apartments of Altgeld Gardens. City officials immediately proposed a plan to remove the materials.

Obama felt triumphant as a result of this win and reflected on it in his memoir:

> I changed as a result of that bus trip. . . . It was the sort of change that's important not because it alters your concrete circumstances in some way. . .but because it hints at what

Obama worked successfully with residents of Chicago's Altgeld Gardens housing project (pictured in 2005) to eliminate cancer-causing asbestos materials.

might be possible and therefore spurs you on, beyond the immediate exhilaration, beyond any subsequent disappointments, to retrieve that thing that you once, ever so briefly, held in your hand. That bus ride kept me going, I think. Maybe it still does.[18]

From Kenya to Boston

Although Obama began to experience more victories than defeats in Chicago, he believed that he needed additional education to become more effective as a leader. So after several years as a community organizer, he decided to apply to law school. He explains what he imagined law school would teach him:

I had things to learn in law school, things that would help me bring about real change. I would learn about interest rates, corporate mergers, the legislative process; about the way businesses and banks were put together; how real estate ventures succeeded or failed. I would learn power's currency in all its intricacy and detail, knowledge that would have compromised me before coming to Chicago but that I could now bring back to where it was needed . . . back to Altgeld; bring it back like Promethean fire.[19]

As he had hoped, Obama was accepted into Harvard Law School.

Before leaving for Boston to attend Harvard, Obama decided to travel to Kenya to learn more about his family. He spent time with aunts, uncles, and cousins whom he met for the first time, and he had the opportunity to meet his Kenyan grandmother, Onyango Obama. All of these relatives told him stories of his father and grandfather. According to author and acquaintance Scott Turow, it was in Kenya that Obama "managed to fully

Before entering law school, Obama visited relatives in Kenya, including his grandmother Onyango Obama (pictured in 2004).

embrace a heritage and a family he'd never fully known and come to terms with his father, whom he'd long regarded as an august foreign prince, but now realized was a human being burdened by his own illusions and vulnerabilities."[20]

Upon his return from Kenya in the fall of 1988, Obama entered Harvard Law School. He excelled there and became the first African American president of the prestigious *Harvard Law Review* in 1990. During this time his potential as a political leader was obvious, especially to his professors, including Laurence Tribe, who taught constitutional law. In an article in *Time* magazine, Tribe states, "I've known Senators, Presidents. I've never known anyone with what seems to me more raw political talent. He [Obama] just seems to have the surest way of calmly reaching across what are impenetrable barriers to many people."[21]

While on leave from Harvard to work as a summer associate at a downtown Chicago firm, Obama met Michelle Robinson. Robinson, also a graduate of Harvard Law School, had earned her undergraduate degree at Princeton University, where her brother was a basketball star. She came from a working-class African American family in Chicago. *New Yorker* staff writer William Finnegan states, "[Obama] turned out to have little interest in corporate law but plenty of interest in Michelle."[22] After their engagement Obama visited Kenya again, this time with Robinson.

Obama graduated magna cum laude (with highest honors) from Harvard Law School in 1991 and was sought after by several prominent law firms. Moreover, Abner Mikva, former five-term congressman for Illinois who was chief judge of the U.S. Court of Appeals for the D.C. circuit, tried to recruit Obama as a clerk, a position "considered a stepping stone to clerking on the Supreme Court,"[23] according to Finnegan. But Obama turned down the judge. Unlike many people in his situation who would have chosen the pursuit of money and power, Obama wanted to return to the roots he had put down in Chicago's South Side.

Back to Chicago

After graduating from Harvard Law School, Obama married Robinson in 1992. The ceremony was bittersweet for the couple:

The *Harvard Law Review*

Published since 1887, the *Harvard Law Review* is one of the most prestigious journals of legal scholarship in the country. It was created by Louis Brandeis, a Harvard Law School alumnus and Boston attorney who went on to become a justice on the U.S. Supreme Court. The purpose of the *Harvard Law Review* is to be an effective research tool for practicing lawyers and students of the law. Additionally, it provides opportunities for law students to write their own articles, which typically take the form of comments about cases or recent court decisions. Run by students, the monthly *Harvard Law Review* averages two thousand pages per volume and reaches eight thousand subscribers, an audience comprising attorneys, judges, and professors.

Each year about ten candidates run for the position of president. Members of the review then elect the candidate best qualified to lead the publication. It is an extremely competitive process. Before Barack Obama in 1991, no African American had ever attained the position, which has served as the launching pad for the careers of some of the most prominent legal minds in America.

Obama is pictured following his election as president of the Harvard Law Review.

In a 2004 photo, Obama and his wife Michelle relax with their daughters.

Robinson's father died before he could give his daughter away, and "Gramps," Obama's maternal grandfather, had recently lost his life to prostate cancer. The newlyweds moved into the Hyde Park neighborhood on Chicago's South Side. They eventually had two daughters: Malia, born in 1999, and Sasha, born in 2001.

As a Chicago resident once again, Obama became director of the Illinois Project Vote, helping register one hundred thousand mostly minority, low-income Democratic voters from April to November 1992. His efforts helped Bill Clinton carry Illinois in the 1992 presidential election, and Carol Moseley-Braun become the first African American woman to be elected to the U.S. Senate.

In 1993 a small public-interest law firm hired Obama. There, he worked as a civil rights attorney, specializing in employment discrimination, fair housing, and voting-rights litigation. That same year he was named in *Crain's* magazine's list of "40 under 40" outstanding young leaders in the city of Chicago. He also became a lecturer at the University of Chicago Law School.

In 1996 Obama's political career was launched when he ran for and won election to the Illinois state senate. As a state senator, Obama focused his efforts on helping working families. One way he did this was to collaborate with Democrats and

All's Fair

In 1996 state senator Alice Palmer offered Obama his chance to run for state senator in the thirteenth district, where he and Michelle lived. Palmer had decided that she wanted to run for Congress, but when she lost the primary election to represent her party, she changed her mind and decided to seek reelection as a state senator. Obama, whose campaign was already in full swing, declined to step aside, claiming that Palmer promised him she would not seek reelection. When Obama's supporters challenged Palmer's petitions, she withdrew and ended her political career.

Some political activists in the state felt that Obama was overly ambitious and should have stepped aside and allowed the more experienced senator to continue the effective work she was doing, Obama was not eager to discuss Palmer, telling a *Chicago Sun-Times* reporter in 2004, "My preference would be not to revisit it too deeply," he says. "But I can tell you that it was an unfortunate situation, but one in which I operated completely aboveboard."

Quoted in Scott Forneck, "Obama: 'I've Got a Competitive Nature,'" *Chicago Sun-Times*, October 3, 2004.

Republicans alike to create programs such as the state earned-income tax credit. A refundable tax credit that reduces or eliminates the amount of taxes that low-income people pay, in three years this program provided more than $100 million in tax cuts to families in Illinois. Obama also pushed through an expansion of early childhood education and helped broaden a state health insurance program for children who were otherwise uninsured.

Crushed by Rush

After nearly four years of serving as a state senator, Obama attempted to become a member of the U.S. House of Representatives by running against incumbent Bobby Rush in 2000. Rush was active during the civil rights movement of the 1960s and was popular among local residents. In 1968 he helped found the Illinois Black Panther Party, a radical group whose occasional militaristic activities attracted the attention of the government and local law enforcement. Rush, however, had also helped his fellow inner-city residents through peaceful and law-abiding means. His record showed improvements in health care and the environment as well as the passage of strong gun-control measures and the implementation of programs that spurred economic development.

Indeed, Rush had been successful in accomplishing many of the social reforms that Obama had been seeking to enact. Yet more important than Rush's seniority and track record was the perceptual advantage he held over Obama. According to Noam Scheiber, Rush's frequent intimations that Obama was not "black enough . . . that he [hadn't] been around the first congressional district long enough to really see what's going on,"[24] and that Obama was an elitist, were difficult to combat. There was little Obama could do to reverse these perceptions, and Rush defeated him, receiving 61 percent of the vote to Obama's 30 percent.

Ups and Downs in the State Senate

After losing to Rush, Obama refocused his attention and talents in the Illinois state senate. Yet even there he suffered a significant political setback. The Republicans were prepared to fight strongly against a gun-control bill, and the Democrats needed Obama's skills and influence to help their side. At the time, Obama was in Hawaii visiting relatives, when his younger daughter became sick. Torn between his obligations to his family and the state senate, Obama chose to stay in Hawaii, and the bill was defeated. Obama's explanation for his absence, according to Turow, "did not play either with the press . . . or his fellow politicians, who'd left plenty of sickbeds and vacations in their time for the sake of public duty."[25]

In 2000 incumbent Bobby Rush (seen in 2006) soundly defeated Obama in the Illinois congressional election.

Nevertheless, Obama carried on in the state senate. He worked to make sure that certain ethnic or minority groups were not unfairly targeted for criminal prosecution and to prevent wrongful convictions in death-penalty cases. After a number of inmates on death row were found innocent, Obama, with the help of law enforcement officials, drafted legislation that required the videotaping of interrogations and confessions in all murder cases. Obama explains some of the benefits of such legislation in a *Daily Herald* article: "Rather than impeding law enforcement, it has made it more simple to prosecute criminals and ensure accuracy in their prosecution."[26] Even as opponents cited the plan as too costly for most police departments, Obama's proposal was approved.

Obama remained fearless in embracing unpopular causes. David Mendell reports in the *Chicago Tribune* that Obama was "one of just nine senators to vote against a bill that toughened penalties for violent crimes committed during gang activity." Obama opposed the bill because the law did not clearly define a gang member, and he questioned why lawmakers were "targeting Hispanics and blacks for stiffer sentences."[27]

Obama also wrote and worked hard to gather support from both political parties for a bill that required law enforcement personnel to keep track of the race of drivers they pulled over for traffic stops. According to Finnegan, this was not necessarily a wise political move because stopping racial profiling was "not a popular issue outside minority communities."[28]

Yet it was precisely the type of issue that Obama seemed uniquely suited to address, and his career progressed unabated. With his abilities as a lawmaker growing, and wiser from his ill-advised run at the House of Representatives, Obama next set his sights on the U.S. Senate.

Chapter 3

Senator Obama

As Obama prepared to take his career to the national level, he had no way of knowing that he was about to benefit from circumstances beyond his control. Even though he had earned an education from two of the best colleges in the country and had worked hard at the grassroots level to gain practical experience, he was aided as well by his political opponents' missteps, which helped clear the way for him to become a U.S. senator.

Setting the Stage

Ironically, in order for Obama to become only the third African American to be elected a U.S. senator, Carol Moseley-Braun, the second African American and the only African American woman ever elected senator, had to make some mistakes. Born and educated in urban Chicago, Moseley-Braun had held local political positions for six years, but her one term in the Senate was marked with controversy. Although never convicted, Moseley-Braun was plagued by allegations of misappropriating campaign expenditures. She and Kgosie Matthews, her fiancé and campaign manager, were accused of using campaign funds to take long and costly trips to places including South Africa, Nigeria, and Hawaii. These travels appeared to be more personal than political. The accusations, along with widespread reports about sloppy bookkeeping, damaged Moseley-Braun's reputation and opened the door for a Republican challenger named Peter Fitzgerald in the 1998 Senate election.

In a state such as Illinois, which largely votes Democratic, it was unlikely that a Republican like Fitzgerald could defeat

Moseley-Braun. But because of the stories about Moseley-Braun's accounting troubles, Fitzgerald, who promoted himself as an outsider to Illinois politics, was able to defeat Moseley-Braun 51 percent to 47 percent, thus becoming the first Republican senator from Chicago in twenty years.

Fitzgerald, an independent thinker, drew criticism from his own party for not supporting more staunchly conservative positions on issues like the environment. For example, he was against exploratory oil drilling in Alaska. He also argued for the appointment of an independent U.S. attorney to investigate corruption in Illinois state government, which resulted in the eventual indictment of Republican governor George Ryan. These beliefs and actions made Fitzgerald an outsider in his own party. Sensing this, he declined to run for a second term as senator. Therefore,

On election night in 1998, incumbent senator Carol Moseley-Braun crosses her fingers for luck, but loses to challenger Peter Fitzgerald.

Moseley-Braun's mistakes and Fitzgerald's maverick personality set the stage for a memorable campaign for the open Senate seat in 2004.

The Senate Democratic Primary

Still a state senator, Barack Obama decided to run for the national position, but he was not favored to win the Democratic primary. Initially, Marson Blair Hull Jr., a businessman turned politician, was the leading Democratic candidate. Hull made millions of dollars selling his investment company, the Hull Group, to Goldman Sachs, a global investment bank. His wealth enabled him to contribute more than $28 million of his own money to his campaign, which gave him a substantial lead in the polls, mostly because of an expensive advertising blitz.

Illinois comptroller Dan Hynes was another Democratic candidate. Hynes came from a powerful political family and had the support of labor unions, which traditionally were part of the so-called machine that exerted great clout during Illinois elections. Conventional wisdom held that to win an election, a candidate had to gain the support of labor union leaders, who then directed union members how to vote. Therefore, by getting the support of one union leader, a politician would theoretically be earning thousands of votes. However, according to David Axelrod, Obama's campaign manager, "A few creaky parts [of the machine] still work. . . . They can still elect a few water commissioners or sub-circuit-level judges. But no precinct captain [from a labor union] can tell people how to vote for President or the Senate."[29]

As he campaigned against Hynes and Hull, Obama began to use his biracial heritage to advantage. He could connect with urban blacks and at the same time build a rapport with suburban and rural white voters, which was unprecedented for a minority candidate. Furthermore, Obama earned support from what William Finnegan called "lakefront liberals—residents of the city's swankier boroughs, most of them white professionals."[30] One reason why this influential, well-educated, and politically savvy group favored Obama was his outspoken opposition to the war in Iraq.

Leaving a Chicago church after an appearance during his 2004 U.S senate campaign, Obama stops to give his daughter a kiss.

Despite growing interest in and support for Obama, he was trailing Hull late in the campaign until a story surfaced alleging that Hull had physically abused his former wife. These charges hurt Hull politically, and his lead over Obama shrank. At the same time, Obama secured endorsements from prominent leaders such as former Democratic national chairman David Wilhelm as well as from the *Chicago Tribune* and the *Chicago Sun-Times*. Campaign manager Axelrod crafted an advertising strategy that drew parallels between Obama and beloved Illinois Democrats, including the late senator Paul Simon and the late Harold Washington, Chicago's first black mayor. Because of the scandal surrounding Hull and the momentum created by his own campaign, Obama won the primary held in March 2004, earning 53 percent of the vote, more than all of the other Democratic candidates combined.

Jack Ryan

Winning the Democratic primary was only half the battle, however; next would come the general election and a formidable Republican opponent named Jack Ryan. Like Hull, Ryan had used

Pictured after winning the Republican nomination for the Illinois senate, Republican Jack Ryan is poised to face Democrat Barack Obama in the general election.

a great deal of his own money to finance his primary campaign. And like Obama, Ryan was young, handsome, and Harvard educated. He had earned a master's degree in business administration from Harvard Business School and a law degree from Harvard Law School. Moreover, like Obama, Ryan did more than talk about helping the underprivileged in urban Chicago. Ryan left his lucrative finance job with Goldman Sachs to teach at an inner-city Chicago parochial high school.

Yet despite their similarities, Ryan and Obama were vastly different in terms of political philosophy. Ryan, more so than even most conservative Republicans, believed in cutting taxes for all citizens, especially high-income earners. He was against gun control and abortion and in favor of school vouchers, which would enable parents to send their children to school districts other than their own to take advantage of better school systems.

Ryan portrayed himself as being consistent in his beliefs in part because he thought he could unearth inconsistencies in Obama's voting record. He also tried to catch Obama making contradictory promises on the campaign trail. Ryan ordered Justin Warfel, a young campaign staffer, to follow Obama everywhere he went and videotape his statements. The objective was to capture Obama on videotape saying one thing to one audience, then promising the complete opposite to another audience. The tactic backfired, however, after Warfel was observed shouting questions in Obama's face and recording Obama's personal conversations with his wife and daughters.

Ryan's Scandal

Ryan's campaign fell apart when lurid details about his relationship with his former wife, actress Jeri Ryan, became public. A popular celebrity in her own right because of starring roles on television shows such as *Star Trek: Voyager* and *Boston Public*, Jeri married Ryan in 1991. The couple had a son, but their demanding careers began to take a toll on their marriage. With Jack in Chicago and Jeri living in Los Angeles, frequent separations caused them to drift apart. They divorced in 1999, five years before the U.S. Senate campaign.

The couple agreed to release divorce papers to the public but requested that child custody files be kept private to protect their son from harm. However, the *Chicago Tribune*, in conjunction with WLS-TV and the local ABC affiliate, conducted an investigation into rumors surrounding the Ryan divorce and pressed the court for more information. In a controversial decision on June 22, 2004, a California judge agreed to release the custody files to the press against the wishes of Jack and Jeri Ryan. The documents contained sexually explicit details about the couple, and the media seized upon the scandalous content, which ruined Ryan's campaign and forced him to withdraw his candidacy for senator. This left the Illinois Republican Party scrambling for a replacement to take on Obama, who was already leading in the polls against Ryan but was now suddenly running unchallenged.

In Comes Keyes

With no Republican challenger to Obama, the Illinois State Republican Committee went beyond state borders to recruit a nationally known African American conservative named Alan Keyes. By this time, Obama's popularity was surging, so Keyes faced an uphill battle trying to convince Illinois residents to vote for him, especially given the fact that he did not even live in their state. Ironically, in 2000 Keyes had publicly criticized former First Lady Hillary Rodham Clinton for running for senator of New York since she was not a native of the state and had only recently moved there. Nonetheless, Keyes accepted the invitation to run against Obama in Illinois despite the fact that he lived in Maryland.

As an African American conservative, Keyes has always drawn attention to himself, which has both helped and hurt his career. Race has invariably been a major issue for Keyes because he rejects many beliefs on race, education, equal rights, and religion that are widely held by other African Americans. For example, Keyes is against affirmative action, a policy that requires state-funded institutions, such as universities and government agencies, to accept or hire a proportionate number of minorities. Furthermore, he has often complained that the media does not give him enough coverage because of his race and views. In an interview on the political television program *Crossfire*, Keyes stated, "I don't correspond to the stereotype, so they're pushing me out. A conservative black American is somebody who simply doesn't correspond to what the media believes black people ought to be."[31]

Yet it was precisely because of his conservatism that the Illinois State Republican Committee believed he could challenge Obama, whose more liberal opinions made for a sharp contrast between the two candidates. In fact, one of Keyes' strategies, much like Ryan's, was to portray Obama as radically liberal on the major issues. Bill Pascoe, Keyes' spokesman, compared Obama's political leanings to other well-known Democrats:

Alan Keyes

Alan Keyes' career included a stint in the U.S. State department, diplomatic positions in India and Zimbabwe, and several important ambassadorial jobs. But Keyes truly came to be known during his failed run for the Republican presidential nomination against George W. Bush and Senator John McCain in 2000. Although he had little chance of defeating either opponent, Keyes managed to remain in the campaign long enough to be invited to participate in several nationally televised debates. The country had not seen an African American politician voice such staunchly conservative opinions before, and many viewers were impressed with him. After bowing out of the election, he parlayed his sudden fame into a talk radio career with his own show, *Alan Keyes Is Making Sense*. The show did not last long, but it enabled Keyes to air his controversial opinions and kept him in the national spotlight until the Republican Party of Illinois asked him to run against Obama.

Were [Obama] to be elected to the United States Senate, he would be to the left of Hillary Clinton on abortion, left of Ted Kennedy on health care, to the left of John Kerry on taxes, to the left of Howard Dean on the war. It will be one of the goals of the Keyes campaign in the last four weeks of this campaign to focus on Barack Obama's [voting] record and make sure the voters of Illinois have a chance to make an informed choice.[32]

Confronting Keyes

Keyes made the mistake of airing controversial opinions about political and lifestyle issues, including religion, which is a subject that is usually excluded from politics. A devout Catholic, Keyes immediately attracted attention by focusing on divisive issues such as abortion and homosexuality. Keyes called abortion a "genocide" of blacks in the United States. He compared the act of abortion to terrorism, saying, "What distinguishes the terrorist from the ordinary warrior is that the terrorist will consciously target innocent human life. What is done in the course of an abortion? . . . Someone consciously targets innocent human life."[33]

Keyes also used religion to attack his opponent. He was quoted in the *Chicago Tribune* as saying that "Christ would not vote for Barack Obama because Barack Obama has voted to behave in a way that is inconceivable for Christ to have behaved,"[34] referring to votes Obama cast in the state senate against antiabortion legislation.

According to staff reporters John Chase and Liam Ford in the *Chicago Tribune*, Keyes even went so far as to declare that "any Roman Catholic who votes for Democrat Barack Obama would be committing a mortal sin. . . . There [is] no difference between Catholics who support Obama and Germans who voted for the Nazi Party."[35] Yet while Keyes kept making shocking statements about his opponent within Illinois, Obama was about to be catapulted from obscurity into the national spotlight.

Recruited to replace the disgraced Jack Ryan in the Illinois senate race, controversial Republican candidate Alan Keyes (pictured) would lose the election to Obama.

"The Audacity of Hope"

By the summer of 2004 John Kerry, a senator from Massachusetts, had taken the lead in the Democratic race and was about to face President George W. Bush in the general election. At the time, the Democratic Party had received criticism for not reaching out to African Americans. After meeting Obama, hearing

Following Obama's memorable keynote address at the 2004 Democratic National Convention, Barack and wife Michelle acknowledge a thunderous ovation.

him speak at a fund-raiser in Chicago, and participating in a town hall meeting with him, Kerry was reportedly impressed with Obama's "passion, eloquence, and charisma," according to one of his aides. After Kerry's advisers predicted that Obama could someday be part of a national ticket, Kerry responded, "He should be one of the faces of our party now, not years from now."[36] The Kerry campaign then asked Obama to give the keynote address at the Democratic National Convention in July in Boston.

Obama recognized Kerry's invitation as an honor and a responsibility and wrote a speech that caught the attention of most of the nation. Titled "The Audacity of Hope," the speech was arguably one of the most memorable moments from the convention. In it, Obama spoke about how the nation's strength could come only from unity, not division:

Now even as we speak, there are those who are preparing to divide us, the spin masters and negative ad peddlers who embrace the politics of anything goes. Well, I say to them tonight, there is not a liberal America and conservative America—there is the United States of America. There is not a Black America and White America and Latino America and Asian America—there's the United States of America. The pundits like to slice-and-dice our country into Red States and Blue States; Red States for Republicans, Blue States for Democrats. But I've got news for them, too. We worship an awesome God in the Blue States, and we don't like federal agents poking around in our libraries in the Red States. We coach Little League in the Blue States, and yes, we've got some gay friends in the Red States. There are patriots who opposed the war in Iraq, and there are patriots who supported the war in Iraq. We are one people, all of us pledging allegiance to the Stars and Stripes, all of us defending the United States of America. In the end, that's what this election is about. Do we participate in a politics of cynicism, or do we participate in a politics of hope?[37]

Dreams from My Father, Thanks to My Mother

After he was made president of the *Harvard Law Review*, Obama was given the opportunity to tell his story in a memoir titled *Dreams from My Father: A Story of Race and Inheritance*, published in 1995. But it was not until his electrifying speech at the Democratic National Convention in 2004 that interest in Obama's life story and sales of the newly released paperback edition skyrocketed. In the book Obama describes his life growing up and evaluates his place in the world as the son of a Kenyan father.

Obama lost his mother to cancer soon after the 1995 edition was published. In the preface to the 2004 release he writes, "I think sometimes that had I known she would not survive her illness, I might have written a different book—less a meditation on the absent parent, more a celebration of the one who was the single constant in my life. . . . I know that she was the kindest, most generous spirit I have ever known, and that what is best in me I owe to her."

Barack Obama, *Dreams from My Father: A Story of Race and Inheritance.* New York: Three Rivers, 2004.

Political experts and many notable politicians weighed in favorably on Obama's performance. He exited the convention and handily won his own election against Keyes, receiving a whopping 70 percent of the vote while Keyes mustered only 27 percent. According to an analyst writing in the *Economist*, "Republicans may try to blame the result on Alan Keyes, their candidate who was hopeless; they may talk about the meltdown of the state's Republican Party; but they lost the race for the open Senate seat in Illinois for a much simpler reason. In Barack Obama, they were up against a star."[38] Obama's victory put an end to a long and bizarre Senate campaign that left many victims in its wake.

On January 4, 2005, Obama was sworn in as a senator and a member of the 109th Congress as family and friends looked on from the visitors' gallery. Many people considered Obama's victory as luck because of the misfortunes of his running mates. Although some of Obama's hardworking staff objected to this view, Obama himself said, "There was no point in denying my almost spooky good fortune."[39]

Chapter 4

Obama and the Issues

Since achieving a landslide victory to become the junior senator of Illinois, Obama has already become an influential voice on Capitol Hill. As a rising star of the Democratic Party, he has often been asked to comment on the policies and actions of George W. Bush's Republican administration. Yet while he has at times been an outspoken opponent of the president's decisions, Obama is also proving that his knack for working with members of the opposition party in the state of Illinois was no fluke. His ability to communicate and compromise is making a difference in the national debate on the most critical international and domestic issues of the day.

Against the War in Iraq

No issue today is as large as the war in Iraq, and Obama has always vehemently opposed it. The Bush administration began the war in March 2003 in the belief that Iraq possessed weapons of mass destruction capable of threatening world peace and that the country's leader, Saddam Hussein, an oppressive dictator who ruled his people through intimidation and violence, was also harboring terrorists.

Before the United States invaded Iraq, there was uncertainty about the U.S. military's ability to effectively defeat Hussein's troops without many American casualties, particularly in the capital city of Baghdad, where a bloody standoff was predicted. However, Iraqi troops were overcome in a matter of weeks with relative ease, and Hussein's regime toppled. Images of an enormous statue of Hussein being yanked to the street by a jubilant mob of Iraqi citizens marked the high point of the invasion. Although Hussein himself fled the capital, he was eventually captured and put on trial as a war criminal.

Yet while the Bush administration was successful in defeating Hussein, no weapons of mass destruction have been found. Furthermore, no link has been established between Hussein and the terrorist group al Qaeda, which is led by Osama bin Laden, the mastermind behind the September 11, 2001, attacks on the World Trade Center and the Pentagon.

Worse, the war continued after Hussein's capture, but it was not waged on a traditional battlefield with identifiable enemy lines; instead, it was fought in a terror zone where numerous insurgent groups seemed to detonate bombs and shoot at U.S.

In a 2006 photo in Washington, D.C., Capitol Hill police surround protesters demonstrating against the war in Iraq, a conflict Obama has opposed from the beginning.

troops daily. In fact, fewer than one hundred American soldiers were killed before Hussein was taken into custody. But as of mid-2006, more than twenty-five hundred had been killed, and the episodes of violence as Iraq scrambled to form its own democratic government dragged on with no end in sight. What was once an apparent victory had turned into a complex mess of warring tribes, with security far from certain. In a speech to the Chicago Council on Foreign Relations on November 22, 2005, Obama stated, "It has been two years and seven months since the fall of Baghdad and any honest assessment would conclude that the Administration's strategy has not worked."[40]

During the buildup to the war in Iraq, the U.S. Senate had voted in favor of an invasion. Although Obama was not yet in office, he opposed the action. He expressed his views in a 2005 speech:

> I think . . . that the [Bush] Administration launched the Iraq war without giving either Congress or the American people

Speaking before the Chicago Council on Foreign Affairs in 2005, Obama calls for troop reductions in Iraq.

the full story. . . . I strongly opposed this war before it began, though many disagreed with me at that time. Today, as Americans grow increasingly impatient with our presence in Iraq, voices I respect are calling for a rapid withdrawal of our troops, regardless of events on the ground. But I believe that, having waged a war that has unleashed daily carnage and uncertainty in Iraq, we have to manage our exit in a responsible way—with the hope of leaving a stable foundation for the future, but at the very least taking care not to plunge the country into an even deeper and, perhaps, irreparable crisis. I say this not only because we owe it to the Iraqi people, but because the Administration's actions in Iraq have created a self-fulfilling prophecy—a volatile hotbed of terrorism that has already begun to spill over into countries like Jordan, and that could embroil the region, and this country, in even greater international conflict.[41]

Obama's predictions about the spread of violence and conflict in the region as a result of the continued chaos in Iraq seemed to be coming true in the summer of 2006. With neighboring Iran disregarding calls from the United States and the United Nations to dismantle its nuclear program and war waging between Israel and Lebanon, it appeared that relations between countries in the Middle East and the United States could be strained even further. Obama is playing a role in international diplomacy as a member of the Senate Foreign Relations Committee, which means that he has the potential to be a key player in future negotiations between the United States and countries that threaten world peace.

The Lugar-Obama Act

One important issue that affects the security of the planet is the potential proliferation of weapons of mass destruction. To maintain world peace, countries must work to remove the threat—specifically, the materials used to produce the weapons. According to Obama, the country that warrants the most attention is Russia, the former Soviet Union. He and others believe that the country's stockpiles of enriched uranium, the key element used to create

During their 2005 trip to Russia, Senators Richard Lugar and Barack Obama visit a Ukrainian warehouse containing defused shells and land mines.

nuclear weapons, could fall into the hands of terrorists. In a speech to the Council on Foreign Relations in November 2005, Obama expressed his concerns:

> Right now, rogue states and despotic regimes are looking to begin or accelerate their own nuclear programs. . . . Some weapons experts believe that terrorists are likely to find enough fissile material to build a bomb in the next ten years—and we can imagine with horror what the world will be like if they succeed. Today, experts tell us that we're in a race against time to prevent the scenario from unfolding. And that is why the nuclear, chemical, and biological weapons within the borders of the former Soviet Union represent the greatest threat to the security of the United States—a threat we need to think seriously and intelligently about in the months to come.[42]

To accomplish these goals, Obama has worked closely with Senator Richard Lugar, a Republican from Indiana who coauthored the Nunn-Lugar Act (1991), which in turn led to the Cooperative Threat Reduction Program. Since its formulation, the program has brought about the deactivation and destruction of 6,828 nuclear warheads, 865 nuclear air-to-surface missiles, 29 nuclear submarines, and 194 nuclear test tunnels as well as thousands of intercontinental ballistic missiles. Obama has become Lugar's Democratic counterpart on recent amendments and expansions to the program.

Obama and Lugar traveled to Russia in 2005 and spent time in Ukraine and Azerbaijan, two states on the fringe of the former Soviet Union, where nuclear, chemical, and biological weapons were created and stored. Obama has observed that because of antiquated technology, old yet dangerous conventional weapons in Ukraine will take sixty years to be properly dismantled. In the meantime, it is entirely possible that such weapons could be distributed to violent pockets in Asia and Africa, where terrorists or rogue governments would welcome the chance to unleash them.

In an effort to prevent such makeshift weapons manufacturing, Obama has worked with Lugar to draft S.2566, the Lugar-Obama

Act. Introduced on April 6, 2006, its purpose is to expand the state department's ability to detect and stop weapons and the development and trafficking of materials to create weapons of mass destruction. Specifically, the act would help secure lightweight antiaircraft missiles. The state department estimates that as many as 750,000 of these shoulder-fired air defense systems are in arsenals worldwide and that more than 40 civilian aircraft have been hit by such weapons since the 1970s.

The potential threat of materials in the hands of terrorists is just one of the major international issues on which Obama is focused. Another is the seemingly separate yet actually intertwined subject of energy and oil production, perhaps the most vital matter affecting American peace and economic prosperity.

The Price of Power

Russia and the Middle East are often the focal points of U.S. foreign policy because these regions produce the vast majority of the world's oil, the lifeblood of the nation's economy. Oil fuels nearly all of the transportation in the United States, yet very little of this oil is produced domestically. This has created an unhealthy dependence on foreign oil, which has led to troublesome compromises with Arab nations that are not ideologically aligned with the United States. And those nations that are supposedly American allies in the Middle East are subjected to terrorist activities targeting oil supplies.

Obama's approach to solving the U.S. dependence on foreign oil is two-pronged: reduce consumption and fund initiatives to rapidly develop alternative fuel sources. He is a proponent for the advancement of biofuels such as ethanol as well as other technologies that harness fuel from agricultural products, including corn stalks and switch grass. He says, "With technology we have on the shelves right now and fuels we can grow right here in America, by 2025 we can reduce our oil imports by over 7.5 million barrels per day—an amount greater than all the oil we are expected to import from the entire Middle East."[43]

In November 2005 Obama introduced legislation called the Healthcare for Hybrids Act (S.2045), which offsets the health

In 2005 Obama introduced the Healthcare for Hybrids Act, to encourage America's "Big Three" auto makers to manufacture hybrid vehicles such as this Ford Escape.

care costs that are choking the profitability of America's "Big 3" automakers: Ford, General Motors, and Chrysler. As part of the pension plan negotiated by labor unions, these companies are obligated to pay for health care benefits for their retired employees, which costs about fifteen hundred dollars for every car sold. This is a financial burden that competitors in countries with nationalized health care systems and nonunionized labor do not have to bear. Obama's plan would provide funding to cover health care costs for automakers that opt to manufacture hybrid vehicles that run on a combination of petroleum and electricity, which reduces gasoline use. In return, the manufacturers would need to invest at least half of the money they save in health care costs in technologies that reduce petroleum consumption, including alternative or flexible-fuel vehicles and hybrids. Manufacturers would also be required to retrain workers and retool their manufacturing plants. Obama explains the measure as a win-win proposal for the industry: "Their retirees will be taken care of, they'll save money on health care, and they'll be free to invest in the kind of fuel-efficient cars that are the key to their competitive future."[44]

Automotive economist Walter McManus sees the bill the same way Obama does, describing it as "a stroke of genius . . . bold, out

Expanding Coal Use

In June 2006 Obama and Senator Jim Bunning introduced the Coal-to-Liquid Fuel Promotion Act of 2006. If passed, the legislation will create tax incentives for coal-to-liquids (CTL) technology and the construction of CTL plants, making CTL an environmentally friendly energy resource in the United States.

Coal is an abundant domestic resource. When gasified in the CTL process, it is refined into diesel. This final product is cleaner than regular diesel because of the removal of sulfur and nitrogen. According to Obama:

> The people I meet in town hall meetings back home would rather fill their cars with fuel made from coal reserves in Southern Illinois than with fuel made from crude reserves in Saudi Arabia. We already have the technology to do this in a way that's both clean and efficient. What we've been lacking is the political will. This common sense, bipartisan legislation will greatly increase investment in coal-to-liquid fuel technology, which will create jobs and lessen our dependence on foreign oil. Illinois Basin Coal has more untapped energy potential than the oil reserves of Saudi Arabia and Kuwait combined. Instead of enriching the Saudis, we can use these reserves to bring a renaissance for Illinois coal.

Barack Obama: U.S. Senator for Illinois, "Senators Obama and Bunning Introduce Legislation to Expand Coal Use," press release, June 7, 2006. http://obama.senate.gov/ press/060607-senators_obama_and_bunning_introduce_legislation_to_expand_ coal_use/index.html.

of the box thinking."[45] In addition to developing incentives to make more fuel-efficient cars, which would have a positive impact on the environment, Obama is trying to enact legislation that would provide government funding for technologies to produce alternative fuels that could reverse the effects of global warming.

Hot About Global Warming

Many scientists believe that Earth's climate is changing in dangerous ways, a future problem that Obama is tackling now. The changes result from the excessive consumption of fossil fuels, used in practically every building, factory, home, and motor vehicle on the planet. The emissions from these fuels create a "greenhouse effect" that allows heat from the Sun to reach Earth but then traps infrared radiation escaping from Earth's surface. In theory, this will lead to higher-than-average temperatures that will cause the coldest places on the planet, such as the North Pole, South Pole, and Greenland, to lose huge portions of ice. As ice melts and breaks loose into the oceans, water levels around the world will rise so that coastlines are gradually submerged by an ever-growing sea. Additional problems may include abnormally warm temperatures that alter plant and animal life within various ecosystems and more frequent and more powerful tropical storms and tornadoes, which derive their strength from warm, wet climates.

Obama has been critical of the Bush administration's skepticism about global warming. He points to countries that are accepting global warming as scientific fact and are changing their lifestyles to reverse the effect. He reminds people of Japan's efforts in slowing oil consumption by making and buying millions of fuel-efficient cars and Brazil's commitment to investment in biofuels, approaches he advocates for the United States, which would increase the volume of renewable fuels required to be blended into a gasoline. Such fuels are derived from sources such as plants or come from the conversion of solar energy into chemical energy.

Obama offers ways in which the government can make investing in alternative energy more attractive, such as forming an energy technology program within the defense department that could provide loan guarantees and funding for plans that develop and market biofuels commercially. Such a plan would decrease the risk inherent in investing in speculative technologies and yet-to-be-established markets. He also advocates several other actions, including setting a renewable fuel standard and creating an alternative diesel standard, with the goal of blending 65 billion gallons of alternative fuels per year with the current petroleum supply by 2025. He also believes that the federal government should purchase only flexible-fuel vehicles, and he supports legislation that would ensure that within ten years every new car sold in the United States is a flexible-fuel vehicle. To support that initiative, he recommends giving automakers a one-hundred-dollar tax credit to install flexible-fuel tanks in their cars, which equals the cost of the upgrade.

In the meantime, Obama is pushing for legislation that would reduce harmful emissions from factories and provide incentives for companies to switch over to cleaner energy alternatives such as solar power. He has also made great strides toward supporting the improvement of cleaner ways to burn coal, which is the most abundant source of energy in this country.

Smart on Education

In addition to energy and environmental issues, education is another of Obama's particular interests. A product of two of the best colleges in the country, he recognizes that many students may not be as fortunate as he was. With tuition costs rising at alarming rates, young Americans from the middle- to lower-income classes may not be able to afford college. Parents and students can take out loans, but that means more debt for families to pay off along with other weighty financial obligations such as a mortgage and health care costs.

Obama recognizes these financial hardships and has taken steps to make education more accessible to everyone. In April 2005 he introduced the Higher Education Opportunity Through Pell Grant Expansion (HOPE) Act. Its purpose is to amend the Higher Education Act of 1965 and make college more affordable by increasing the maximum amount of Pell Grant awards from $4,050 to $5,100 a year, nearly 26 percent. It is estimated that more than

Tennis star Venus Williams reads about good dental hygiene habits to students in Head Start, a program that Obama strongly supports.

5 million undergraduate students depend on Pell Grants to help them defray college costs, and 85 percent of Pell Grant recipients come from households with an income below $40,000. Obama described the current problems with Pell Grants at a press con-

Hard Knocks at Knox

During a June 2005 commencement speech at Knox College in Illinois, Obama shared with graduates the importance of a good education in today's economy.

> While most of us have been paying attention to how much easier technology has made our own lives—sending e-mails back and forth on our Blackberries, surfing the Web on our cell phone . . . a quiet revolution has been breaking down barriers and connecting the world's economies. . . . Now business not only has the ability to move jobs wherever there's a factory, but wherever there's an Internet connection. Countries like India and China realized this. . . . They can compete with us on a global scale. The one resource they needed were skilled, educated workers. So they started schooling their kids earlier, longer, with a greater emphasis on math and science and technology, until their most talented students realized they don't have to come to America to have a decent life—they can stay right where they are. The result? China is graduating four times the number of engineers that the United States is graduating. . . . If you've got the skills, you've got the education, and you have the opportunity to upgrade and improve both, you'll be able to compete and win anywhere. If not, the fall will be further and harder than it ever was before.

Barack Obama: U.S. Senator for Illinois, "Remarks of U.S. Senator Barack Obama at the Knox College Commencement," June 4, 2005. http://obama.senate.gov/speech/050604-remarks_of_us_senator_barack_obama_at_the_knox_college_commencement/index.html.

ference at the Southern Illinois University at Edwardsville: "Pell grants, the government's primary financial aid for college students, only cover 23 percent of the total cost of an average four year public institution . . . and they have not been indexed to the rising price of tuition or inflation. As a result, the current limit is worth $700 less than it was worth 30 years ago."[46]

Political Optimist

But it is not only education at the college level that concerns Obama. He is also committed to ensuring full funding of government-sponsored programs such as Head Start, which provide education, medical, dental, and parent-involvement programs to impoverished children and their families. Because of his commitments to early childhood education and to accessible, high-quality day care, Obama was the 2005 recipient of the Harold Blake Walker Award, which is given to individuals for their contributions to human services or social reform.

The next year, in March 2006, Obama introduced S.2441, a bill to authorize resources for the development of twenty so-called innovation districts. These districts would emphasize teacher recruitment, training, and retention, including pay increases to high-performing teachers and financial incentives to teachers willing to work in low-income schools. In a speech titled "21st Century Schools for a 21st Century Economy," Obama points out, "Teaching is one of the only professions where no matter how well you perform at your job, you're almost never rewarded for success."[47] In an innovation district, teachers would be given mentors for more support and more time with their students in the form of longer days or summer school. Those schools that fail to meet predefined expectations would be eliminated from the program.

Whether it is education, energy, the environment, or foreign relations, Obama is focusing his attention and efforts on key domestic and international issues that hold tremendous significance for the future of the United States. Clearly, he is a leader with his vision trained on the horizon. And because of his forward-looking, optimistic approach to politics, many people who are looking ahead to future presidential elections have their eyes on Obama.

Chapter 5

The Challenges Ahead

The Barack Obama story to date remains an unfinished tale. In some ways, Obama seems to be more famous for what he might yet do rather than for what he has actually done. Indeed, despite his many accomplishments thus far, many people believe that his greatest successes are still to come. Therefore, he has become the subject of a great deal of speculation as a politician with unlimited potential, a future leader who could unite numerous contentious factions and bring real change and progress to government, the country, and the world.

Of course, it will be hard to live up to such expectations. His future as a leader is by no means assured. For example, some of his strengths—his heritage, his beliefs, his voting record—could also be construed as political weaknesses that potential opponents will likely exploit. However, time and time again Obama has seemed to say and do the right thing at the right time at each stage of his life. And though people may argue about the future of his career, there is one point on which everyone can agree—Obama is someone worth watching on the American political scene.

Bridging Divides

One of the most repeated compliments made about Obama is that he is able to bring opposing groups together. In Washington, this is known as working both sides of the political aisle, which means that he is capable of collaborating with certain Republican counterparts to win important votes for proposed legislation. This is critically important when a bill founders in committee because Democrats and Republicans cannot agree on an issue. Too often senators are derided for being partisan, voting according to the dictates of their political party rather than on their core personal beliefs or on what is best for the public.

Such partisanship and the overall bureaucracy of government have caused people to lose faith in Washington, says Obama. He explains in his book, *The Audacity of Hope:*

> They [Americans] may still vote, out of habit, anger, or some atavistic sense of civic obligation. But they don't have much confidence that government can do them a lot of good. They

A proponent of bipartisanship, Senator Obama joins Republican senators Tom Coburn (left) and Sam Brownback at a press conference.

African American Senators in U.S. History

Obama's Senate victory in Illinois literally made history, as he became the fifth African American senator in U.S. history and only the third elected since the end of Reconstruction, the period immediately following the end of the Civil War. Federal troops occupied the South after its defeat, and a process was put in place to ensure that newly freed slaves were allowed to vote fairly and freely in elections. At that time members of the U.S. Senate were not directly elected by voters in most states. Instead, they were elected by legislators in the state assemblies or were appointed by the governor. This led to the election in 1870 of Hiram Rhoades Revels, the first black to serve in the Senate, followed by the 1875 election of Blanche K. Bruce. Both men were from Mississippi.

It took more than half a century after the passage of the Seventeenth Amendment, which provided for the direct election of senators by the people of a state rather than their election or appointment by a state legislature, for an African American to earn a Senate seat. In 1966 Massachusetts voters elected Edward William Brooke III, a Republican who served two terms. Fourteen years later Illinois elected Carol Moseley-Braun, who became the first African American woman to serve in the Senate. She served one term, and her seat was later filled by Obama.

Pictured in 1870, Hiram Rhoades Revels was the first African American to become a U.S. senator.

hope, at best, that it does them no harm. . . . A government that truly represents these Americans—that truly serves these Americans—will require a different kind of politics than we have now. . . . We will need to understand just how we got to this place, this land of warring factions and tribal hatreds. And we'll need to remind ourselves, despite all our differences, just how much we share: common hopes, common dreams, a bond that will not break.[48]

The more Obama proves himself to be a senator who can bridge divides between parties, the more his stock rises as a leader. Yet there are more than just political divides that present challenges to Obama. Race, which sometimes works to his political advantage, also looms as one of the biggest obstacles in his political future.

The Race Catch-22

Since the end of the Civil War, only three African Americans have been elected to the Senate. Thus, although the country has made great progress toward equal rights for citizens of all ethnicities, by and large such equanimity has not reached Capitol Hill, where the preponderance of lawmakers are white. Furthermore, only one African American governor has been elected in the history of the United States. As reporter Patrick Reddy points out, "Major party black candidates for president, governor, and U.S. Senator (including Obama) have won just three of 28 contests."[49] Therefore, any African American running for high political office must be considered an underdog who invariably must confront the issue of race in his or her campaign.

According to Noam Scheiber, race has always been an issue for African American political candidates, and it has generally caused their campaigns to take one of two forms. He explains:

The first—what you might call the Bobby Rush strategy—has been to rely either exclusively on African American voters or on a coalition of African American and white liberals, with little attempt to reach white moderates. . . . To win elections in parts of the country where culturally moderate whites are the decisive swing voters—which is to say, most of America—African-American candidates have attempted a second approach: de-emphasizing race and running to the political center.[50]

This presents a unique challenge for Obama if he aspires to higher political office, such as governor of Illinois or even president of the United States. He will have to appeal to both blacks and whites without favoring one side over the other. If he is perceived solely as a black candidate, he could lose white voters; conversely, his appealing to white voters might cause blacks to feel as though he has abandoned them. Scheiber explains, "African-American candidates for statewide office nearly always end up in a catch-22: Attempts to motivate their African-American base usually alienate white moderates. And when black candidates try to tailor their message to white moderates, they dampen enthusiasm among African Americans and liberals."[51]

Obama, in large part because of his mixed heritage, does not face the exact same racial dilemma, but that does not mean that he can avoid race as an issue. Of course, he is not the first minority candidate confronted by this challenge, but because of his mass appeal, he may be the first to actually overcome it.

Cross-Cultural Appeal

Obama's mixed race and excellent communication skills help mitigate the polarizing effect race can have on a politician. More so than any other nonwhite leader in the United States, Obama seems capable of defusing negative opinions about blacks held by whites while simultaneously maintaining ethnic authenticity among African Americans. As noted by Scheiber:

The power of Obama's exotic background to neutralize race as an issue, combined with his elite education and his credential as the first African-American *Harvard Law Review* President, made him an African-American candidate who was not stereotypically African American. . . . Free of the burden of reassuring culturally moderate whites that he wasn't threatening, Obama could appeal to their economic self-interest while also exciting his African-American and progressive white base.[52]

Obama appeals to voters because he takes on issues that affect people of all races in both urban and rural areas, such as jobs, health care, and education. According to Washington correspondent Ryan Lizza of the *New Republic*, "Obama's ability to appeal to inner-city blacks, suburban moms, Republican dentists, and, well, me suggests that he'll be able to venture further than most black politicians."[53] In fact, Obama is so adept at transcending

Both during his 2004 senate campaign (pictured) and today, Obama attracts black and white supporters alike.

race that he may have more problems overcoming the liberal label that has been pinned on him.

The Liberal Label

In the current political environment, when someone is tagged a liberal, it carries with it the suggestion that that person believes in more government programs, which in turn requires higher taxes among citizens. As a liberal Democrat, Obama will have to fend off the negative connotations that come with the liberal label, which could hurt his chances in future elections, but it will not be easy. In fact, since the 1988 presidential election, when conservative Republican strategists stamped Democratic presidential nominee Michael Dukakis as a liberal, the term has done more harm than good for Democrats. However, while some Democrats deny their liberal leanings in fear of losing favor with the public, Obama promotes the value of liberalism. Rather than run from the accusations of favoring government-funded programs, Obama takes a stand against the elimination of government programs designed to help people by improving health care and social security. And according to writer and columnist Anna Quindlen, Obama has "revived the power and the glory of American liberalism just by showing up."[54]

In contrast to those like Obama who hold liberal beliefs, Republicans often advocate privatization, which means that businesses would take over some functions currently carried out by the government. Their reasoning is that the open market, where people decide where to spend their own money, has proved to be very effective for families and the overall economy. For example, American consumers, unfettered by government dictates, determine the supply and demand for goods and services, ranging from homes to automobiles to clothes, food, and entertainment. Moreover, businesses motivated by profit typically move more quickly and efficiently than government programs at virtually all levels, from the federal government to state- and municipally funded programs.

Yet while privatization may work occasionally, Obama believes it does not apply to all arenas. He explains that by advocating a reduction in the size of government and the elimination of depart-

Obama favors government funding for programs that improve the lives of Americans, such as social security, health care, and education.

ments that manage programs such as social security and education, Republicans jeopardize the quality of life for nonwealthy and disadvantaged citizens. He says:

> The reason [Republicans] don't believe government has a role in solving national problems is because they think government is the problem. That we're better off if we dismantle

it—if we divvy it up into individual tax breaks . . . encourage everyone to go buy your own health care, your own retirement security, your own child care, their own schools, your own private security force, your own roads, their own levees. . . . It's called the Ownership Society in Washington. But in our past there has been another term for it—Social Darwinism—every man or woman for him or herself. It allows us to say to those whose health care or tuition may rise faster than they can afford—life isn't fair. It allows us to say to the child who didn't have the foresight to choose the right parents or to be born in the right suburb—pick yourself up by your bootstraps. It lets us say to the guy who worked twenty or thirty years in the factory and then watched his plant move out to Mexico or China—we're sorry, but you're on your own.[55]

Senator Obama, pictured (center, hands folded) with other members of Congress, believes that government programs can foster equality among classes and cultures.

By articulating how government programs can help bring about equality among classes and cultures, Obama could help redefine liberalism in the United States from simply meaning unchecked government taxation and spending to worthwhile government social action. Yet it remains to be seen if that strategy will resonate with a national audience or even to residents within Illinois should Obama forego a second term as senator and run for governor. Such a move might be wise if he aspires to be more than a senator.

Senators and Presidents

History has shown that the longer Obama stays in the Senate, the less likely it is that he will attain higher elected office. That is because very few senators have made it to the White House. Often they are defeated by incumbents or by governors running for the office. Bill Clinton, for example, the incumbent president and former governor of Arkansas, easily defeated longtime senator and former vice-presidential candidate Bob Dole in the 1996 presidential election. More recently, longtime senator John Kerry was beaten by incumbent president George W. Bush, former governor of Texas, in the 2004 presidential election. In fact, only two sitting senators in the last 115 years—Warren G. Harding and John F. Kennedy—have been elected president. As Reddy states, "The Senate once was thought to be the cradle of Presidents. But it has become the graveyard for most national ambitions."[56]

One reason why senators have difficulties in presidential elections is that their voting record in Congress can be used against them by their opponents. Such was the case for Kerry in 2004 when Bush's campaign advisers pointed to a long list of Kerry votes against military spending, which led the public to question Kerry's commitment to the armed forces while the United States was engaged in the war in Iraq. Another reason senators do not fare well against governors as opponents is that governors are perceived as leaders whereas senators are viewed as one vote among one hundred on Capitol Hill. Senators propose and vote on bills to create laws, a critically important facet of a democracy, but governors serve as heads of state and can prove how effective they were in that role. In fact, five of the last seven presidents

—Richard Nixon, Jimmy Carter, Ronald Reagan, Bill Clinton, and George W. Bush—were governors. The other two—Gerald Ford and George H. Bush—were vice presidents hand-picked by presidents Nixon and Reagan, respectively.

A third truism about senators is that they typically remain in the Senate a long time. One term lasts six years; therefore, two terms span more than a decade, and that much time in office usually leads to the public perception that a senator is a Washington insider, someone incapable of relating to the world beyond the Capitol and therefore incapable of changing any perceived problems with Washington. By contrast, governors vying for the White House often portray themselves as Washington outsiders who do not play party politics.

True or not, this strategy tends to work. Should he stay in the Senate too long, Obama's name and reputation could become associated with the government as is, rather than what the government could be, as he so often likes to advocate. Political columnist and author Joe Klein explains the danger of Obama not taking advantage of his current political popularity: "Freshness doesn't last forever. If Obama waits and hangs around the Senate for six to 10 more years, he may wind up sounding like a Senator—which is to say he will no longer have command of the English language—and, worse, he may start thinking like a Washington politician, wizened by the accepted limits of the possible."[57] Yet, for the moment, concerns about Obama being too entrenched in Washington are premature since he is only in his first term in the Senate.

Future Political Aspirations

Obama's current reputation is highly favorable. He possesses a charming personality and is a compelling public speaker, a potent combination that disarms opponents and engages those faithful to him. Amanda Ripley captures why Obama appeals to so many people:

Obama is charismatic, but not in a jovial, Clintonian kind of way. He is intense, surprisingly so. He has a way of telling

The Name Game

One potential obstacle to Obama's chances of winning a national election is his name itself. By mainstream American standards, the name *Barack Obama* is not ordinary. The fact is that the occupants of the White House have always had common Anglo-Saxon last names, from Bush to Clinton, Reagan, Carter, Ford, Nixon, and Johnson, all the way through Truman, Wilson, Adams, Monroe, Madison, and Washington. Odd- or ethnic-sounding presidential names such as Roosevelt, Eisenhower, and Kennedy are rare, which begs the question of whether Americans are ready for someone with a name like Obama in the White House. Obama himself makes light of his name in speeches when he recounts how people mispronounce it or humorously mistake it for phrases like *Yo Mama*. He also recognizes the unfortunate similarity between his name and terrorist mastermind Osama bin Laden's. Yet Obama seems poised to overcome any potential problems surrounding his exotic name, as he has the other hurdles in his way.

Obama pokes fun at his unusual name.

The magnetic young senator charms people with his wit and intelligence.

you something as if it's the only time he has told it to any-one (even if, like all politicians, he is working you with the same line he has used at every ballroom in the state). His brow is almost always furrowed, and his voice is deep, even somber, despite his boyish face. . . . And . . . Obama is a master at shaping his own mythology.[58]

Although Obama has not publicly stated that he aspires to the presidency, there is certainly enough buzz to explore the possibility that he will run someday. An article in the online magazine

Grist claims, "His eventual presidential run is seen as inevitable. He's a phenomenon, and everyone wants to see him up close."[59] Even hall-of-fame rocker Neil Young endorsed a presidential run for Obama in his 2006 song "Lookin' for a Leader."

According to Klein, Obama "isn't not running for President," but as he quickly adds, "this is not to say he has decided to run." Klein goes on to explain:

> The effortlessly charismatic Obama has been besieged by people urging him onward and upward ever since his terrific keynote address at the Democratic Convention in 2004, and he has always demurred. But the discussions have grown more serious in recent months as assorted Democrats, especially some high-powered money people, have surveyed the potential 2008 field and found it wanting.[60]

Others, such as syndicated political columnist Leonard Pitts Jr., caution against putting too many expectations on Obama. Pitts writes, "Yes [Obama] has great potential. But is it asking too much that people wait until he actually does something before they start chasing his name with a hallelujah chorus? Can we at least give him time to figure out where the restrooms in the Capitol are?"[61]

Even Klein recognizes that Obama is "as green as Kermit the Frog. He is a mere 44 years old and has been a member of the US Senate for less than two years. He sits on the Foreign Relations Committee, but he has zero military and national-security experience. He's a very smart guy, a quick learner, but no one is that quick."[62]

Beating the Odds

Yet while the writings of well-informed political reporters hold significance regarding Obama's future, the most telling words on the subject may have come from President George W. Bush. At the 2005 annual Gridiron Dinner, an event where politicians and the media meet to tease one another in a roast forum to benefit charity, Bush addressed Obama directly: "Senator Obama, I want to do a joke on you, but doing a joke on you is like doing a joke on the Pope. Give me something to work with. Mispronounce something."[63]

Hinting that Obama is infallible is high praise, but even though he has managed a startlingly impressive career and has crafted a seemingly impeccable persona, Obama's strengths may lie not in his aura of faultlessness but rather in his unconventional background, which helps him identify with a variety of audiences. His broken home, estranged father, youthful indiscretions, and period of underachievement—typical strikes against candidates seeking national office—are things with which the vast majority of Americans today can relate.

As demographics in the United States continually evolve, the overall mindset of the country seems also to be shifting. With races and classes merging through marriage, immigration, improved access to education, and economic opportunity, the country may be more accepting of someone who does not come from an elite, well-to-do background. Obama has had to rely on his own innate talents and intelligence to overcome obstacles that have ruined the political careers of more privileged candidates. His proven ability to beat the odds has led his allies and opponents to both willingly and begrudgingly agree that he is capable of addressing the major challenges that lie ahead for him and the country. In the meantime, Obama's achievements to date are sure to inspire other people from every culture and class in the United States for years to come.

Chapter 1: A Fateful Beginning

1. Barack Obama, keynote address at the Democratic National Convention, July 27, 2004. www.barackobama.com/2004/07/27/dnc_2004.php.
2. Barack Obama, *Dreams from My Father: A Story of Race and Inheritance.* New York: Three Rivers, 2004, p. 15.
3. Obama, *Dreams from My Father*, p. 17.
4. Obama, *Dreams from My Father*, p. 126.
5. Obama, *Dreams from My Father*, p. 51.
6. Obama, *Dreams from My Father*, p. 52.
7. Obama, *Dreams from My Father*, pp. 69–70.
8. Quoted in *O, the Oprah Magazine*, "Oprah's Cut with Barack Obama," November 2004. www.oprah.com/omagazine/2004 11/omag_200411_ocut.jhtml.
9. Obama, *Dreams from My Father*, pp. 79–80.
10. Obama, *Dreams from My Father*, p. 99.
11. Obama, *Dreams from My Father*, pp. 100–101.
12. Noam Scheiber, "Race Against History," *New Republic*, May 31, 2004.

Chapter 2: The Streets of Chicago

13. Obama, *Dreams from My Father*, p. 115.
14. Obama, *Dreams from My Father*, p. 134.
15. Obama, *Dreams from My Father*, p. 136.
16. Obama, *Dreams from My Father*, p. 139.
17. Obama, *Dreams from My Father*, pp. 164–65.
18. Obama, *Dreams from My Father*, p. 242.
19. Obama, *Dreams from My Father*, p. 276.
20. Scott Turow, "The New Face of the Democratic Party—and America." http://dir.salon.com/story/news/feature/2004/03/30/obama/index.html.
21. Quoted in Amanda Ripley, David E. Thigpen, and Jeannie McCabe, "Obama's Ascent," *Time*, November 15, 2004.

22. William Finnegan, "The Candidate," *New Yorker*, May 31, 2004.

23. Finnegan, "The Candidate."

24. Quoted in Scheiber, "Race Against History."

25. Turow, "The New Face of the Democratic Party—and America."

26. Quoted in Anne Marie Tavella, "Taping Murder Interrogations Wins Early Senate Support," *Daily Herald*, March 5, 2003.

27. David Mendell, "Obama's Record a Plus, a Minus," *Chicago Tribune*, October 8, 2004.

28. Finnegan, "The Candidate."

Chapter 3: Senator Obama

29. Quoted in Finnegan, "The Candidate."

30. Finnegan, "The Candidate."

31. Quoted in Alan Keyes Archives, "Alan Keyes on *Crossfire*," December 15, 1999. www.renewamerica.us/archives/media/interviews/99_12_15crossfire.htm.

32. Quoted in Mendell, "Obama's Record a Plus, a Minus."

33. Quoted in Natasha Korecki, "Keyes Likens Abortion to Terrorism." *Chicago Sun-Times*, August 17, 2004.

34. Quoted in Liam Ford and David Mendell, "Jesus Wouldn't Vote for Obama, Keyes Says," *Chicago Tribune*, September 8, 2004.

35. Quoted in John Chase and Liam Ford, "Keyes Presses Catholic Voters," *Chicago Tribune*, November 1, 2004.

36. Quoted in Jill Zuckman and David Mendell, "Obama to Give Keynote Address," *Chicago Tribune*, July 15, 2004.

37. Obama, keynote address at the Democratic National Convention.

38. *Economist*, "Obama's Second Coming: Victory for a Rising Star," November 6, 2004.

39. Barack Obama, *The Audacity of Hope: Thoughts on Reclaiming the American Dream*. New York: Crown, in press, p. 9.

Chapter 4: Obama and the Issues

40. Barack Obama, "Moving Forward in Iraq," November 22, 2005. http://obama.senate.gov/speech/051122-moving_forward _in_iraq/index.html.

41. Obama, "Moving Forward in Iraq."
42. Barack Obama, "Nonproliferation and Russia: The Challenges Ahead," November 1, 2005. http://obama.senate.gov/speech/051101-non-proliferation_and_russia_the_challenges_ahead/index.html.
43. Barack Obama, "Energy Security Is National Security," February 28, 2006. http://obama.senate.gov/speech/060228-energy_security_is_national_security.
44. Obama, "Energy Security Is National Security."
45. Quoted in HybridCars.com, "The Healthcare for Hybrids Act." www.hybridcars.com/health-care-for-hybrids-act.html.
46. Quoted in Brandee J. Tecson, "Obama's HOPE Act: A Bid to Make College More Affordable," MTV News, April 1, 2005. www.mtv.com/news/articles/1499404/20050401/index.jhtml?headlines=true.
47. Barack Obama, "21st Century Schools for a 21st Century Economy," March 13, 2006. http://obama.senate.gov/speech/06031321st_century_schools-for_a_21st_century_economy/.

Chapter 5: The Challenges Ahead

48. Obama, *The Audacity of Hope*, p. 18.
49. Patrick Reddy, "Obama for President? Rising Democratic Star Faces Major Obstacles on the Road to the White House," *Buffalo News*, March 27, 2005.
50. Scheiber, "Race Against History."
51. Scheiber, "Race Against History."
52. Scheiber, "Race Against History."
53. Ryan Lizza, "The Natural," *Atlantic Monthly*, September 2004.
54. Anna Quindlen, "A Leap into the Possible," *Newsweek*, August 9, 2004.
55. Barack Obama, "Remarks of Senator Barack Obama at Emily's List Annual Luncheon," May 11, 2006. www.barackobama.com/2006/05/11/emilys_list_luncheon.php.
56. Reddy, "Obama for President?"
57. Joe Klein, "Barack Obama Isn't Not Running for President," Time.com, May 28, 2006. www.time.com/time/columnist/klein/article/0,9565,1198859,00.html.

58. Ripley, Thigpen, and McCabe, "Obama's Ascent."
59. David Roberts, "For Those About to Barack," *Grist Magazine*, March 21, 2006.
60. Klein, "Barack Obama Isn't Not Running for President."
61. Leonard Pitts Jr., "Senator Barack Obama Is Not the Savior of Democratic Party," *Olympian* Online, March 20, 2006. http://159.54.227.3/3/apps/pbcs.d11/article?AID=20060320/OPINION/60320016/1005.
62. Klein, "Barack Obama Isn't Not Running for President."
63. Quoted in Anne E. Kornblut, "But Will They Love Him Tomorrow?" *New York Times*, March 19, 2006.

1961

Barack Obama Jr. is born in Honolulu, Hawaii, August 4.

1979–1981

Attends Occidental College in Los Angeles.

1983

Graduates from Columbia University.

1983–1987

Works as a community organizer in Chicago.

1990

Becomes the first African American president of the *Harvard Law Review*.

1991

Graduates magna cum laude from Harvard Law School.

1992

Directs a voter registration drive in Chicago. Marries Michelle Robinson.

1995

Publishes his memoir, *Dreams from My Father: A Story of Race and Inheritance*.

1996

Obama is elected to the Illinois state senate.

1997–2004

As an Illinois senator, he represents the thirteenth district.

2000

Obama runs unsuccessfully in the Democratic primary for Illinois' first congressional district against incumbent representative Bobby Rush.

2004

Gives the keynote address at the 2004 Democratic National Convention in Boston, Massachusetts, on July 27. Obama's memoir is rereleased in paperback.

2005

Obama is sworn in as a U.S. senator for Illinois on January 4. In April he proposes his first Senate bill, the Higher Education Opportunity Through Pell Grant Expansion Act of 2005 (HOPE Act). He also, along with Senator Richard Lugar, drafts S.2566, the Lugar-Obama Act, to expand the state department's ability to combat the creation of weapons of mass destruction. In August he visits Russia as a member of the Senate Foreign Relations Committee with Lugar. In September he begins a downloadable podcast from his Web site.

Books

Marlene Targ Brill, *Barack Obama: Working to Make a Difference.* Minneapolis: Millbrook, 2006. A biography of Obama that discusses his parents, childhood, education, and political and public life. The author offers insights about Obama through interviews she has conducted with some of Obama's colleagues and friends.

James Daley, *Great Speeches by African Americans: Frederick Douglass, Sojourner Truth, Dr. Martin Luther King, Jr., Barack Obama, and Others.* Mineola, NY: Dover, 2006. An anthology of speeches by influential people in the African American community. Some of the speeches included are the famous "Ain't I a Woman?" speech by Sojourner Truth (1851), Martin Luther King Jr.'s "I Have a Dream" (1963), Thurgood Marshall's "The Constitution: A Living Document" (1987), and Barack Obama's "Knox College Commencement Address" (2005).

Barack Obama, *The Audacity of Hope: Thoughts on Reclaiming the American Dream.* New York: Crown, 2006. In this book, Obama recounts his early experiences as a senator and explains his vision of more authentic politics.

———, *Dreams from My Father: A Story of Race and Inheritance.* New York: Three Rivers, 1995. In this memoir, Obama discusses his life growing up with his mother and grandparents in Hawaii and his struggles to connect with his African heritage and identity despite the absence of his Kenyan father. The time period covered in this book includes Obama's life from birth through college, his early career as a community organizer, and his postgraduate education at Harvard Law School. A full copy of the speech he gave at the Democratic National Convention is included in a rereleased 2004 paperback edition.

Web Sites

Barack Obama: U.S. Senator for Illinois (http://obama.senate. gov). What Obama calls his "online Senate office," this site provides

Obama's podcasts, speeches, and press releases. It also posts up-to-date Senate news and information on important events going on across the state of Illinois.

Knox College (www.knox.edu/x9683.xm). This site includes a video and transcript of Obama's 2005 commencement speech at Knox College in Illinois.

On the Issues: Every Political Leader on Every Issue (www.on theissues.org/Senate/Barack_Obama.html). This Web site provides nonpartisan information for voters. It also gives information about Barack Obama's and other legislators' views and voting records on issues such as homeland security, foreign policy, crime, civil rights, tax reform, social security, technology, abortion, and education.

U.S. Senator Barack Obama (www.barackobama.com/main.php). Obama's official campaign site. It provides a video of Obama's speech at the Democratic National Convention and also includes press releases, news, and links to news articles on the Web.

WashingtonPost.com: The U.S. Congress Votes Database (http://projects.washingtonpost.com/congress/members/o00016 7/key-votes). This site publishes the results of congressional votes on the most important bills, nominations, and resolutions that have come before the 109th Congress, as determined by WashingtonPost.com. Republican and Democratic majority opinions for each piece of legislation are also shown.

Mark and Sherri Devaney are married writing partners who seek inspirational topics to write about and found one in *Barack Obama*, their second Lucent book. Mark, a former teacher and journalist, is a business development professional for an engineering firm. Sherri is an editor who focuses on educational and medical publishing. They live in Sparta, New Jersey, with their biggest inspirations, Sean and Jeremy.